Insight for Children

4–5 Years Book C, Modules 29 and 30

General Editor: David G. Hamilton

Contributors: David G. Hamilton, Elsa Hamilton

Marshall Pickering
An Imprint of HarperCollinsPublishers

Marshall Pickering is an Imprint of
HarperCollins*Religious*
Part of HarperCollins*Publishers*
77–85 Fulham Palace Road, London W6 8JB

First published in Great Britain
in 1997 by Marshall Pickering

1 3 5 7 9 10 8 6 4 2

© 1997 David G. Hamilton

David G. Hamilton asserts the moral right to be
identified as the author of this work

A catalogue record for this book is
available from the British Library

0 551 030844

Printed and bound in Great Britain by
Woolnough Bookbinding Limited, Irthlingborough, Northamptonshire

Contents

Introduction   iv

MODULE 29:   **ALL GOD'S PEOPLE**

Session 1   The Tent of God   2

Session 2   Joshua does as he's told   4

Session 3   The great little army   6

Session 4   Friends that couldn't be separated   8

Session 5   Solomon builds a Temple   10

Session 6   God is real   12

Session 7   Save the people!   14

Session 8   Daniel's courage   16

MODULE 30:   **JESUS AND HIS FRIENDS**

Session 1   Come and meet Jesus   20

Session 2   The brothers follow Jesus   22

Session 3   Sickness in the family   24

Session 4   A friend in high places   26

Session 5   The importance of asking questions   28

Session 6   The man who changed his ways   30

Session 7   No gift is too great   32

Session 8   When friends let us down   34

Introduction

INSIGHT is the learning programme for the whole Church. Within the programme, the *INSIGHT for Children* series serves the needs of those within the age range 4–11 years. Over the first four years of the *INSIGHT for Children* series, a total of 24 volumes of Leader's Notes will be published at the rate of six per year, two volumes in each of the three age bands. Each volume will offer a total of 16 learning episodes and these will be arranged either in two modules of eight episodes each or in three modules comprising one of eight episodes and two of four episodes each. This means that for each age band there will be 32 new episodes appearing each year. These learning sessions provide enough by way of guidelines and specific resource ideas for one session lasting anything from 30 minutes to one hour. For each volume of Leader's Notes there is a companion volume of children's activity papers.

The age bands suggested in the *INSIGHT for Children* series have been set notionally as follows:

4–5 years
6–8 years
9–11 years

The reasoning behind these suggested age groupings is set forth in chapter 4 of the *INSIGHT Handbook*. It is stressed, however, that these are simply recommendations. The essential thing to note is that there are no hard-and-fast rules here. If congregations elect to structure their age bands along the lines of, say, 5–7 years, 8–9 years, 10–11 years, or indeed any other realistic combination, then the system will operate just as well.

It is to be hoped that the *INSIGHT for Children* series will be used as a means of integrating children and young people into congregational life. The general slogan of the *INSIGHT* programme as a whole, 'For Membership through Membership', is of particular significance for those in their earliest years. It is our primary objective to give our children enjoyable, encouraging and meaningful experiences of the congregation as a faith community. Full attention needs to be paid, not simply to the content of a learning session, but to the way in which it is presented, the friendliness of the group and indeed the whole ambience of the Church experience. The educational and pastoral roles of those who work with children in the Church cannot be separated. In short: we not only teach the love of God, we need to demonstrate that love.

THE STRUCTURE OF THE WEEKLY PROGRAMME

This second-year volume of Leader's Notes (Volume C) provides structures for the learning sessions in modules 29 and 30 for the 4–5s. (There is a second volume available for modules 31, 32 and 33.) Each learning session is structured along easy-to-follow conventional lines. Look out for the following main headings:

Calling all leaders
Off we go
Worship tips

Calling all leaders offers preparatory notes for the leader. These include sections on *Our goal, Bible focus* and *Get organised*. They provide a clear and solid foundation for your presentation. Always take time to work through this situation well in advance.

Off we go offers a shape for your presentation based upon the earlier preparation. It has been organised in a series of steps. The *step-by-step* approach will help you not only to give clear shape to your presentation but will help you to check as you go that you are progressing in an organised and helpful way.

These presentation notes are simply guidelines. They need not be taken verbatim. It is important for the leader, especially in story-telling, to read the Notes, summarise them, possibly into a number of headings to be used as prompts, and, having assimilated the key ideas, present the session in her/his own words. Eye contact with the children and an easy rapport with them are of central importance.

Worship tips is not a comprehensive diet of worship: it simply offers some ideas and suggestions pertinent to the theme for the session. Leaders are encouraged to incorporate these ideas into the worship periods prepared by them. With children in the early school years the provision of a worship table is recommended. This should be used to provide a thematic focus for both the lesson and the worship. It is best if the ideas offered in the learning sessions are used in a brief final act of worship in which the essential point of the lesson is expressed in prayer, song, dance, mime or other art form.

SHORT OF TIME?

It is well recognised that in some congregations Sunday School groups meet on Sunday morning during the hour of congregational worship when, usually, the children are present in church for a period before leaving for their own group meeting in adjacent premises. For these groups time is short and many of the lesson plans may require to be curtailed. The *step-by-step* plan allows leaders to omit one or more steps according to the time available. In each learning session provision is made for the selection of key steps, marked by an asterisk (*). Unmarked steps, it is suggested, should be excluded from the presentation only if absolutely necessary.

Wherever possible, groups should try to give maximum time for these learning sessions. This is discussed in the *INSIGHT Handbook*, chapter 4, but several brief observations are worth making here. The options open to leaders at the stage of planning the events include:

- *extending a learning episode over two sessions*
- *increasing the teaching/learning time available*
- *reviewing how best time can be used in the group by recognising how easy it is to waste time with preliminaries, administration, failing to set out the work areas beforehand and needless verbosity*
- *avoiding introductory worship with the group when the children have already worshipped in the church service and, instead, letting them go straight to work groups.*

Careful management will save an astonishing amount of time for effective group work and in many instances will obviate the need to reduce the published learning plans.

ACTIVITY PAPERS

Activity papers are available for the children and these should be regarded as essential to the programme, as leaders will be continually referred to exercises in these papers which are tightly integrated into the lesson structures. There is an attractive, four-colour, four-page activity paper corresponding to each learning session. The intention is that each child should be in possession of an activity paper on the occasion of each meeting of the group. These activity papers serve two purposes. They summarise for the children the key ideas in the teaching programmes. They also engage each child in activity work designed to foster understanding. Many of the activities are intended to be completed within the session when the group is together; other activities are intended to be completed at home. Leaders are urged to consult the activity paper for a learning session well in advance and as an essential part of their preparations.

PLANNING AND PREPARATION

It is of the utmost importance that the leadership team should meet in advance of the commencement of a module to plan their presentations in the ensuing weeks. This will require the leaders to review the module theme as a whole and to grasp the vision offered by the topic.

At a practical level there is much to be done in terms of:

- *finalising a timetable*
- *identifying things to do in advance*
- *allocating responsibilities for specific tasks, including the sharing of the leading of worship*
- *identifying the need for resource materials and ensuring that these are to hand when they are required.*

In addition to the collective planning of the group there is the need for the individual leader or teacher to prepare each learning event in advance. Leaders are advised to review the materials for a forthcoming lesson early in the preceding week and to ensure that they are organised for the presentation.

THE MODULES AT A GLANCE

Module 29: All God's people

This module features eight well-known heroes and heroines of the Old Testament. Through them, the story of God's purposes worked out in the history of Israel is portrayed in a series of 'snapshots' suitable for this age band. It is a demanding module in that it introduces new names and – for some at least – new stories, to the children. It is important, however, if our children are to grow into a knowledge of the Bible, that we should make a beginning. Hopefully this module will help build a basis for future understanding.

Module 30: Jesus and his friends

This module provides more familiar territory for younger children, based upon the experience of friendship. In these sessions, the children are introduced to various gospel characters such as Philip, Nathaniel, James and John, Simon's family, Matthew the tax collector, Mary, Martha and Lazarus and many others. The module allows us to create a backdrop for future reading and understanding of the gospels. Once again, much emphasis is placed on the familiarisation of the children with names and ideas outside their immediate experience, while seeking to relate these to their own world.

RESOURCES

Details of the volumes to which reference has been made are provided below, together with details of other books which may prove useful.

The Church Hymnary, Third Edition (Oxford University Press, London), 1973.

Big Blue Planet, ed. Judy Jarvis (Stainer & Bell and Methodist Church Division on Education and Youth, London), 1995.

Children's Praise, compiled Greg Leavers and Phil Burt (Marshall Pickering, London), 1991.

Junior Praise, compiled Peter Horrobin and Greg Leavers (Marshall Pickering, London), 1986.

Sing to God, compiled Margaret V. Old and Elspeth M. Stephenson (Scripture Union, London), 1971.

Someone's Singing, Lord, compiled Beatrice Harrop (A & C Black, London), 1973.

Songs of God's People, compiled John Bell (Oxford University Press), 1988.

Good News Bible (The Bible Societies and Collins, London), 1976.

DAVID G. HAMILTON
GENERAL EDITOR

MODULE TWENTY-NINE

All God's people

The Tent of God

Our goal

Our goal will be to help the children explore the origins of the Church through the story of Moses and the people of God as they travel with the Tent of the Presence of God.

Bible focus

Exodus 25:1–2, 8–9; 26:1–36
Before the Hebrews settled in fixed locations and before the first Temple was built, the people of God carried with them on their travels the *Tent of the Presence of God*, also known to us as the Tabernacle. Whenever they set up camp, the Tent was set up in the midst of the community. The origins of the practice are attributed to Moses (see Bible readings listed above), although it is certain that the whole cultic system of worship and sacrifice and the role of the priests were subject to considerable development over a number of centuries. Eventually, the more substantial Temple replaced the Tent and thus the styles of worship were developed and refined still further. Yet, from the very beginning, there was the belief that God was always in the midst of his people.

Get organised

This session focuses on God at the centre of his people, always and everywhere. The idea of a travelling people, camping and trekking, should be developed using camping equipment, simulated experiences with tents, etc. Pictures from bible encyclopaedia may prove useful in establishing the idea of the Tent of God at the heart of a campsite. Compare this with a picture of a church at the heart of a village. Keep storylines such as the creating of the Tent or the giving and storing of the Ten Commandments *very* simple.

Things you may need

- [ ] activity papers and crayons/paints/pencils
- [ ] small tent with weights to hold guy ropes
- [ ] pictures from bible encyclopaedia and of a local church.

Step 1

Let the children talk about the pictures of camping and different kinds of tents on page 1 of the activity paper. Draw upon their experiences. Say that we are going to learn about the Tent of God.

Step 2

The idea of taking your home with you as you travel around the country is best approached from the modern experience of camping holidays and caravan

trips. Use magazine clippings and other pictures to establish the idea. You might even unpack and repack a bivouac tent as a demonstration. (Practise in advance!) You may even leave the tent up during the lesson. Emphasise that the tent is portable.

Step 3*

Talk about the people of God moving around the country long ago. There were thousands of them, led by Moses. Everywhere they went they carried their tents and all their belongings. Invite the children to imagine what that must have been like. How would they travel? (Bus, car, train? Camel and donkey?) Ask them to imagine the tribe of people as a village, settling in one place for months – sometimes years – then moving on to another place.

Stress that, just as we have churches in our towns and villages, they had the Tent of God, where people came to praise God. The big difference was that everywhere they went they had to take their 'church' with them!

Step 4*

Refer to page 2 of the activity paper. Talk about the Tent in general terms. (The details of Exodus 26 are not relevant for this age group.) Make the point that the Tent was always at the centre of the tented village.

Step 5*

Talk about God's promise to his people: 'I will be your God and you will be my people'. Ask the children to colour in the words and to learn them as they do so.

Step 6

In the Tent of God the special box (the Box of the Covenant) was kept, and in that box the ten rules for living in a way that pleased God were kept. Every person among God's people had to learn these rules and live by them. (There is no need with this age band to teach the Ten Commandments in specific terms.) Go over with the children the four bullet points on page 3 of the activity paper.

Step 7*

Talk about the rule to do with God's special day. We now call it Sunday, the day we worship God together in Church. Let the children talk about the pictures on page 3 of the activity paper.

Step 8

Talk with the children about going to church on Sunday. Use page 4 of the activity paper. Let the children draw a picture of the inside of their church.

WORSHIP TIPS

Song

'Lord Jesus, be thou with us now', No. 16, *The Church Hymnary 3*; 'Round and round the circle', No. 22, *Big Blue Planet*.

Bible

Exodus 25:8–9

Prayer points

- Give thanks to God for your local church and those who built it.
- Ask God to be present in your group as he was with his people long ago.
- Pray for people who spend much of their time travelling, for their safety and that they might be aware of God's presence.

Joshua does as he's told

Our goal

Our goal is to introduce the younger children, using the story of Joshua, to the idea that God has a purpose for his people and that this requires our obedience and faith.

Bible focus

Joshua 6:1–21
The details of Joshua 6–9 make gruesome reading, by any standards. At one level this story has all the elements of religious imperialism at its cruellest. To the modern reader, the actions of the Israelite army are indefensible. But we have to set aside our modern perspective and see the story as an example of the obedience and faith which the people of Israel believed necessary to please their God; and that occupying the promised land was accomplishing God's purposes. It is a philosophy that has reverberations to this day in the politics of the Middle East. In the context of the story of faith, we can only view the period in terms of a people who sought God's will and tried to carry it through in a way that was commonplace in their time and generation. We may identify with the motives, if not with the deeds, of Joshua! The use of the story with children should be restricted to a fun level – circling the city of Jericho and identifying Joshua as an important leader of God's people.

Get organised

Use Joshua 6:1–16 as the basis for the story you will tell. Know the biblical text well and rework it into a simple format for the younger children. Plan for a *safe* mime of the battle of Jericho. If possible, have some of the items prepared in advance. Prepare a simple script to be read over the mimed actions. Start gathering lots of cardboard boxes!

Things you may need

- [ ] activity papers and crayons/paints
- [ ] newspaper, cardboard, adhesive tape
- [ ] cardboard boxes
- [ ] large box
- [ ] copy of 'Trumpets of God' from *Insight for Children*, 4–5 Years Book B (Activity Papers), Module 4, Session 1.

Step 1

Use page 1 of the activity paper to lead a conversation on 'doing what we are told'. Establish the idea that sometimes we are told to do things even when we don't *yet* understand the reasons for doing them. In years to come these reasons will become clear to us.

Step 2*

Tell the story of Joshua, the general of the Israelite army, based upon Joshua 5:13–6:16. The storyline might be thus: Joshua meets a strange warrior who turns out to be God's messenger; Joshua is instructed to set his army against the city of Jericho, to capture it and destroy it; the plan is to march around the city on each of seven days; seven men, each with a huge battle trumpet, march in front of those carrying the Box of God, with the soldiers marching behind; on the seventh day there is a blast on the trumpets and a great shout from the army, so loud that the walls of the city collapse; Joshua's army enters the city as victors.

Emphasise the ritual circling of the city seven times and the effect of the great sound of trumpets and voices, all as God had commanded Joshua.

Step 3*

Work through with the children the revision questions on page 2 of the activity paper, correcting, reinforcing and elaborating on the story as you go.

Step 4

Let the children colour the picture of the priest with the great battle trumpet on page 3 of the activity paper. Talk about the picture and how the trumpet was used to strike fear into the enemy.

Step 5*

Enable the children to make simple trumpet shapes from card or paper as shown on page 3 of the activity paper. These may be used later. Let the children make simple paper helmets (from newspaper, for example), and simple, blunt, cardboard swords, both for the defenders and attackers of the city, for use in the next step.

Step 6*

Organise with the children the building of 'the city of Jericho' from cardboard boxes, arranged to create a rampart all around the people of the city. Divide the group into attackers and defenders. The attackers will need their trumpets. They should also carry around the city a large cardboard box to represent the Box of God.

Prepare a simple narrative script to read the story of the battle of Jericho and let the children mime the story as you tell it.

Use the slogan of Joshua's army at the end as Joshua acknowledges the cheers of his warriors: 'The Lord has given you the city'.

WORSHIP TIPS

Song

'We all march to the beating drum', No. 76, *Big Blue Planet*; 'There's a fight to be fought', No. 159, *Sing to God*; 'Trumpets of God', *Insight for Children*, 4–5 Years Book B (Activity Papers), Module 4, Session 1.

Bible

Joshua 6:16

Prayer points

- Ask God to help us to do what he would have us do.
- Thank God that he is with us always.
- Pray for peace among all the peoples of the earth, that all wars may end.

The great little army

Our goal

Our goal in this learning session is to help the children to recognise the name of Gideon as one of the heroes of God's people and how, through the story of his victory, we recognise that great achievements may spring from small beginnings in the purposes of God.

Bible focus

Judges 7
Gideon was one of the judges (that is, charismatic leaders) of ancient Israel. He is best remembered for the manner of his defeat of the Midianite and Amalekite tribes – marauding Arabs who rode in from the desert and attacked the Israelite settlements. The thrust of the tale as a story of faith has to do with God's insistence that Gideon should not rely on strength of numbers but upon the inspiration of the Spirit in achieving his purposes. Through the story, as in others in this series, there runs the conviction that Israel are God's people, specially chosen to achieve his purposes in history. This is their mission; however, it requires obedience to the will of God and a trust that God is with them in all circumstances. The reduction in the number of Gideon's troops is meant to be read in that light. We resist the temptation to liken Gideon's fighting force to an SAS elite squadron of modern times!

Get organised

This session stresses the potential for great achievements arising out of small beginnings and small numbers. Make much of Gideon's natural inclination to think big and God's word to him to cut his numbers. Prepare the story and the battle mime to afford the children maximum participation and fun. If possible, use the battle materials from Session 2 together with torches and such like required for this session.

Things you may need

- [ ] activity paper and crayons/paints
- [ ] paper helmets, swords and trumpets (possibly from session 2)
- [ ] torches.

Step 1

Let the children talk about the pictures on page 1 of the activity paper. Draw out the idea that small creatures and tiny people can have a big effect on others much bigger than them.

Step 2*

Use page 2 of the activity paper to introduce the figure of Gideon. Use the paper interactively, feeding information into the conversation and drawing from the children their own observations. Make a lot of the destruction and misery caused by the marauding Midianites.

Step 3*

Use the text on page 3 of the activity paper as a *basis* for telling the story of Gideon's war. Use your own words and capture the children's imaginations. Talk about the battle picture on the activity paper.

Step 4

Let the children act out the story of Gideon's war. Note that the trumpets, helmets and swords used for Session 2 may be reused here (if they have survived!). Use the war cry: 'A sword for the Lord and for Gideon!'

Step 5

Under the slogan 'small beginnings lead to great things', create a frieze showing items such as seeds and flowers, acorns and trees, baby bootees and huge adults, etc. Use magazine pictures and/or natural objects.

Step 6*

Use page 4 of the activity paper to bring forth from the children suggestions as to how they as 'little people' can bring great joy and help to grown-ups.

Step 7

Let the children colour the words of the war cry. Talk about how Gideon's victory over the desert warriors saved his country and helped God's plan to unfold.

WORSHIP TIPS

Song

'Glory to our wonderful God', No. 54, *Big Blue Planet*; 'Hands to work and feet to run', No. 465, *The Church Hymnary 3*.

Bible

Judges 7:2

Prayer

Lord, we are your little people and you are our great God. Give us hearts to love you as we love others and hands to help you in helping them.
Amen.

Friends that couldn't be separated

Our goal

Our goal in this session is to explore the notion of friendship through the story of David and Jonathan and to identify David as a great leader of God's people and friend of God.

Bible focus

1 Samuel 17:34–51; 20:17–42
The story of David as told in 1 Samuel is full of passion and heroic action. At one level it is about the heights of human greatness and the depths of human frailty. At a deeper level it is about God's purpose being worked out in the life of David. David will become King of Israel and Emperor of a vast surrounding territory. His son, Solomon, will inherit and expand even further a massive and wealthy kingdom. David represents the high point of Israelite success. For young children it is enough that they should recognise David as a great and heroic figure of the Bible and of the story of faith.

Get organised

A successful approach for this session depends on the appeal to the imagination of the children through well-told stories and effective reflection on the characters of the story. The technique of inserting the correct word in a sentence (see page 2 of the activity paper) is by no means impossible, but does require patience and so cannot be rushed; much of the material must be both read and written for the children. It does, however, provide a useful conversation method which will challenge the child to think about the storyline. Remember that it is through the internalising of words and stories that the child's ability to understand will develop.

Things you may need

- [ ] activity papers
- [ ] pencils/crayons/paints.

Step 1

Use page 1 of the activity paper to talk about the children's best friends. Talk about the qualities of best friends and let the children make their drawing in the space provided. Use the opportunity to develop the notion of friends together in church.

Step 2*

Talk with the children about David and Goliath. Find out from the story how much they know already. Correct and/or fill in the blanks. In some cases these may be considerable, but persevere with the approach. Use pictures from children's illustrated bibles, if you wish.

Step 3

Now go over the story again, this time using page 2 of the activity paper. Help the children to fill in the missing words. You may have to print these. The exercise may take time but remember there is no merit in rushing this kind of learning approach. Draw attention to the selection of 'missing' words listed on the page. You might say 'Is it hero?', or 'Is it King?'. Then read the correct version of the story, with all the blanks properly filled in. Talk about the picture on the page.

Step 4*

Using the text on page 3 of the activity paper as a basis, tell in your own words the story of David and his friend Jonathan. Stress that from the time David defeated Goliath he was popular with the people, even more popular than King Saul. Tell in the most vivid way possible the story of how Jonathan saved David's life.

Step 5

Let the children colour the story picture and talk with them about the action. Who fired the arrows? Why? What was the signal? What did David do?

Step 6*

Prepare the way for children and parents to talk at home by referring to the information on page 4 of the activity paper. Talk about friendship and very best friends. Tell how David went on to be a great King and of how he wrote lots of songs of praise to God.

Step 7

Teach the words of the song, 'Jesus is a friend of mine'.

WORSHIP TIPS

Song

'Jesus is a friend of mine', No. 136, *Junior Praise*, 'I'm sitting by myself', No. 73, *Big Blue Planet*.

Bible

2 Samuel 5:1–3

Prayer

Use the words of the hymn 'Jesus, Friend of little children', No. 100, *The Church Hymnary 3* as a prayer.

Solomon builds a Temple

Our goal

Our goal in this session will be to show the children how King Solomon used his wealth to build the first Temple as a house of God, and how nothing but the best and most beautiful is fit for the place where we worship God.

Bible focus

1 Kings 6
The details of the extravagance and sublime beauty of Solomon's Temple are quite breathtaking. Consider the period in history, the labour force required, the standard of craftsmanship, the procuring of raw materials and the architectural genius in its design. It ranks among the greatest wonders of the ancient world yet served 'only' the purpose of worship. That is an awesome and humbling thought. The Temple was built for and to the glory of God. That is the definitive statement on the high watermark of the civilisation of ancient Israel. It begs questions of our own civilisation!

Get organised

Gather photographs from magazines of new buildings of all shapes and sizes. Include churches and other places of worship. Concentrate on variety. Take time to read about Solomon's Temple, set in the midst of a prosperous Israelite empire. Focus also on beauty. This session can easily be expanded by inviting the children to engage in various expressive activities such as painting, modelling and singing – all ways of praising God.

Things you may need

- [ ] activity papers and pens/pencils
- [ ] crayons or paints
- [ ] materials for additional expressive activities.

Step 1*

Talk with the children about new buildings. Use page 1 of the activity paper as a stimulus. Talk about church buildings in general and your own church building in particular. How long did it take to build?

Step 2

Refer to page 2 of the activity paper and recall with the children the earlier session on the Tent of the Presence of God which travelled with the people on their journey. Show how, in time, the people settled down in towns and villages. Talk about the jobs people did and their places of work.

Step 3*

The biggest city was Jerusalem, where King Solomon lived in a very fine palace. Solomon was the son of the famous King David. He was very wealthy and very powerful. He was also a man who loved God and so he decided that he would build a special building where God would be worshipped. It would replace the Tent.

Step 4*

Refer to page 3 of the activity paper. Solomon's special building was called the Temple. Let the children talk about the pictures on the activity paper and any other pictures you have which show what the Temple was like, both inside and outside. If you have access to any models of the Temple this would be useful. Use the information on this page to develop for the children some idea of how very special the Temple was for the people of God.

Step 5

King Solomon insisted that the house of God should be very beautiful. It should have nothing but the very best of wood and gold, curtains and perfumes. Let the children say why they think this should be. Lead them to see that in Solomon's time, nothing but the very best was fit for God.

Step 6*

Let the children explore your own church building and encourage them to pick out one item that they think is beautiful. Let them draw and colour this on the activity paper on a larger sheet. Let the children share their stories of why they chose their items. Draw together those items as signs of beauty in your church.

WORSHIP TIPS

Song

'This is God's holy house', No. 18, and 'All things bright and beautiful', No. 154, both from *The Church Hymnary 3*.

Prayer

Lord of all beauty and power, we praise you. Your presence among us thrills us and makes us want to sing and pray and speak of your greatness. Accept not only the worship of our voices but also of our hands, our hearts and our lives.
Amen.

God is real

Our goal

Our goal in this learning session will be to identify Elijah the prophet as a famous leader of the people of God and, through the story of the 'contest of the gods' on Mount Carmel, to show how in a time of unbelief Elijah demonstrated the powerful presence of the living God.

Bible focus

1 Kings 18
This is a story about drought and rain! It begins with a severe famine in the land of Israel after the death of Solomon, and after the kingdom had split following dreadful civil war. The northern kingdom of Israel was ruled by King Ahab, whose wife, Jezebel, was a worshipper of the pagan god, Baal. Most of the prophets of the Lord God had been killed at the whim of Jezebel. Elijah was among the few who survived. Our story tells of how the famine became the occasion for a contest between the prophets of Baal and the prophet of God, Elijah. Elijah's prayers are answered and the long sought after rains come in the postscript to one of the greatest stories in Scripture.

Get organised

This session focuses on Elijah on Mount Carmel. The storyline is dramatic and should be fully exploited. Prepare well. The teaching point is that the Lord alone is God. God should come first in our lives, always. Much of the organisation and preparation will lie in being able to cope with this central idea in conversation. Work through the activity papers thoroughly in advance.

Things you may need

- [ ] activity papers and pens/pencils
- [ ] pictures of mountain scenes and mountain activities
- [ ] crayons or paints.

Step 1*

Use page 1 of the activity paper to introduce the topic of hills and mountains. Let the children talk of their experiences of the hills. Show how there are stories in the Bible which feature mountains (Moses, Noah, Jesus).

Step 2*

Introduce to the children the character of Elijah, the special messenger of God (avoid the word prophet). Use page 2 of the activity paper as the basis for a storyline, based upon 1 Kings 18.

Step 3*

Let the children colour the picture on page 3 of the activity paper. As they do so, use conversation to revise the story and to bring out the main point that God made himself known to all the people in answer to the prayer of Elijah.

Step 4*

For Elijah, there was nothing more important than God. For many people today, as in Elijah's time, there are other things they think are more important. Based upon the section in page 4 of the activity paper, let the children talk about the three pictures showing what is important to some people. Develop the conversation on what is important and what is not.

Step 5

Tell the children about the teaching of Jesus: that we should put God first in our lives. In much the same way that is what Elijah was saying all those years ago.

Step 6

Let the children colour the letters of Elijah's special message. Encourage them to learn the words and to know who first said them.

WORSHIP TIPS

Song

'Let us sing our song of praise', No. 625, *The Church Hymnary 3*; 'Let us praise God together', No. 14, *Sing to God*.

Bible

1 Kings 18:37–39

Prayer

Lord, you alone are God. We praise you. We want to be your people, always. Make us strong to stand up for you and ready always to tell of your goodness.
Amen.

Save the people!

Our goal

Our goal in this learning session, using the story of Esther, is to encourage in the children the attitude of acceptance of all people as being equal in the sight of God and to counteract the development of social and religious prejudice.

Bible focus

Esther 1–7
At one level this is sexist stuff! Esther, the beautiful Jewess, goes out of her way to capture the heart of the king and succeeds admirably. Such is the power of her beauty, her charm and her guile that she soon rises from the status of concubine to replace the old queen. From this position, Esther learns of Haman's plot against the Jews and exerts influence over her husband to rescind the order of execution. At a deeper level, the book of Esther is yet another example of the stories of faith, whereby the purposes of God are worked out in the history of the Jewish nation, even in captivity in Babylon.

Get organised

Young children are very easily influenced to adopt attitudes of social and religious prejudice and we have a duty to set the record straight. God has no favourites. You may have an ethnic mix in your group of children, or at least a mixture of children from the nations of the UK. Use this situation to good effect. Gather photographs and any other materials which point out the cultural and religious differences of people in our society. The lesson is best handled by taking time for an imaginative exploration of our differences (*Step 1*).

Things you may need

- [ ] activity papers
- [ ] photographs of different cultures
- [ ] percussion instruments.

Step 1*

Talk with the children about the different groups of people we see and meet. Some have a different colour of skin, some speak a different language, some dress differently and some have different religions. If possible, use pictures to stimulate conversation. Allow the children to make their observations. Your task here will be to establish that, whatever their differences of appearance and background, all people everywhere are the same in the eyes of God. It is wrong to favour some and not others.

Step 2*

Indicate that the story today has three main characters and that it is set in the palace of the King of Persia. In the country at that time there were many Jewish people. They had been brought there from their own country as slaves.

Introduce the main characters using page 1 of the activity paper – the King of Persia, Esther and Haman.

Step 3*

Using the biblical text (Esther 1–7) as a basis, tell the story of how Esther came to the royal court, how Haman tricked the king into signing the death warrant of all the Jewish people in the land, and how Esther persuaded the king to change his mind and spare the Jews.

Step 4

Using the cartoon strip on page 2 of the activity paper, let the children talk about the story, frame by frame.

Step 5

Explain to the children that ever since the time of Esther, Jewish people have held a special party day to remember how they were saved from death by Esther's bravery. This is called the feast of Purim. (There is no need for the younger children to remember the term!) Refer to the scripture quotation on page 2 of the activity paper.

Step 6*

Refer the children to page 3 of the activity paper. Organise a percussion band and learn the song, 'Thank you, Lord, for this fine day' and possibly the other songs listed. Take time to practise singing, playing, dancing, skipping or marching. Let them have fun in preparation for a joyous worship session.

Step 7*

Finally, take a few moments to go over the points made in the 'Calling all parents' section of the activity paper. The pictures show a Sikh person, a Jewish boy, a Buddhist, rival football fans and a homeless person. Reinforce the point that we need to accept all those who are different from us, just as God accepts them.

WORSHIP TIPS

Song

'Thank you, Lord, for this fine day', No. 232 and 'I've got that joy', No. 121, both in *Junior Praise*; 'You shall go out with joy', No. 120, *Songs of God's People*.

Bible thought

God's people survived Haman's plot to kill all of them. To this day, people remember Esther and her friends.

Prayer

Use the prayer printed on page 4 of the activity paper.

Daniel's courage

Our goal

Our goal in this learning session is to help the children, through the story of Daniel, to learn more of God's readiness to uphold his people.

Bible focus

Daniel 6
The book of Daniel is a strange writing and Daniel is a strange person. He was a Jew, yet held high office in the King's palace and was obviously a favourite. The new rule requiring emperor worship and the exclusion of all other 'gods' put Daniel on the spot. He couldn't possibly comply with this rule and the King couldn't easily retract it. They reached an *impasse* and Daniel was consigned to the pit of lions. The story ends with justice being done on all sides. God kept faith with the man who had kept faith with him.

Get organised

This is an abbreviated lesson based on the much-loved story of Daniel. It should be used to show the justice or unfailing love of God and the protection of his people. The lesson should also be used as a means of gathering in a brief revision period all eight stories pursued in the module. Have copies of all eight activity papers to hand.

Things you may need

- ☐ activity papers
- ☐ pens/pencils and crayons
- ☐ copies of all eight activity papers in this module (for leaders).

Step 1*

Work through with the children the checklist of good rules and bad rules. They may need help in understanding the principle of checklists but should soon catch on. Talk about what makes good rules and bad rules. From their concrete responses try to establish a general principle, such as: 'A good rule will allow people as much freedom as possible without causing difficulty for others' or, more simply, 'It is good to respect other people'.

Step 2*

Use the text on page 2 of the activity paper as a *basis* for telling in your own words the story of Daniel. Emphasise the King's friendship with Daniel the Jew, how the bad rule threatened Daniel's life, how Daniel survived the experience amongst the lions, and how the relieved King changed his mind and made a new rule.

Step 3

Ask the children to look at the picture of lions on page 3 of the activity paper. Talk about what might happen if anyone went into their den. Yet Daniel survived. Now let the children draw the figure of Daniel in the white space in the picture. He is praying to God and the lions ignore him!

Step 4*

Talk about prayer and ask the children what things they might pray about. Let them print a short prayer or draw a prayer picture that they can explain.

Step 5*

Take time at this point to sum up this series of lessons. Recall the names of the eight heroes in our stories. (Refer to the activity paper, page 4.) Using a children's illustrated bible, show how in the stories of the Old Testament God is to be seen working through people.

Show also how, in the Church today, God is at work through his people – people like us!

Step 6

Learn the words of the first verse of the song, 'The Church is wherever God's people are praising'.

WORSHIP TIPS

Song

'The Church is wherever God's people are praising', No. 427, *The Church Hymnary 3*; 'Daniel was a man of prayer', No. 367, *Junior Praise*.

Bible

Daniel 6:25–27

Prayer points

- Thank God for the example of the great men and women of the Bible.
- Ask God to help us be faithful and to be good followers of Jesus, our Lord.
- Give thanks for the Church as the people of God in today's world.

Jesus and his friends

Come and meet Jesus

CALLING ALL LEADERS

Our goal

Our goal in this learning session is to focus on the idea of sharing friendship by introducing friends to each other and to convey the unique quality of friendship experienced by the disciples of Jesus.

Bible focus

John 1:35–42, 43–47; 12:20–26
In the early stage of his ministry, Jesus gathered together a small group who became his disciples. Andrew and Philip first encountered Jesus, and then introduced him to Peter and to Nathaniel. Their enthusiasm and commitment meant that they resolved at once to draw others into the friendship of Jesus. In Jerusalem, near the end of Jesus' ministry, both Philip and Andrew are seen again as the disciples who introduce others to Jesus.

Get organised

Prepare for the mime in *Step 5*.

Things you may need

- ☐ a few photographs of your friends or family friends
- ☐ cardboard rectangles (about 16 cm x 11 cm) with the words of the invitation in the activity paper printed on them
- ☐ camera and film
- ☐ story book about Bambi or Postman Pat or Noddy.

OFF WE GO

Step 1

Show the children the photographs of your friends. Tell them their names, and something about them – particularly anything interesting or funny. Ask the children to tell you about their friends, and why they like them.

Step 2*

Display the picture on the activity paper which shows someone introducing one friend to another. As the children colour it in, talk about it, drawing the children's attention to the fact that you have all been introducing your friends to each other in *Step 1*.

Step 3

Look together at the chosen story book. Read any of the pages which describe the friends of Bambi or Postman Pat or Noddy.

Step 4

Draw the children's attention to the pictures of people saying 'Hello' on page 1 of the activity paper. Act out some of these. (Rubbing noses will probably be more popular than kissing!)

Step 5*

Read the story of Nathaniel meeting Jesus in the activity paper. If possible, try a simple mime, with Philip coming for Nathaniel and bringing him to Jesus. The children could be divided into groups of three for the mime. Talk about how keen Philip was that Nathaniel should meet his friend Jesus.

Step 6*

Take a group photograph of your class. Explain that you will hope to have the film developed and printed for the next meeting of the group.

Step 7*

Think now about inviting a friend to come to church or to Sunday School. Use the cards or cut out the invitation on page 3 of the activity paper and ask each child to print a name of a friend *or* tell you a name which you can print.

Step 8*

Ask the children to draw a picture of their church in the space provided on page 4 of the activity paper. Use the 'Calling all parents' section to go over with the children how God's people of old would carry their churches around with them, rather than having a building to go to, which we have now.

WORSHIP TIPS

Song

'Jesus, Friend of Little Children', No. 100, *The Church Hymnary 3*.

Prayer

Father God,
Today we have been thinking of your friends,
And of Philip and Nathaniel.
Help us to be like them
And to know you as our friend.
Amen.

Bible reading

On the next day, Jesus walked past. John the Baptist was standing with two of his disciples. They both followed Jesus. One of them was Andrew. He had a brother called Simon Peter. He took him to Jesus.

On the next day, Jesus said to Philip: 'Come with me.' So Philip went to look for Nathaniel and took him to Jesus.

John 1:35–42 (adapted)

The brothers follow Jesus

Our goal

Our goal in this learning session is to reflect on the story of two brothers who decided together to give their lives to the friendship of Jesus; and through this to promote the idea of the discipleship of family and of community.

Bible focus

Mark 1:14–20; Luke 10:38–42
The gospels tell us of brothers and sisters deciding together to follow Jesus. Though discipleship is ultimately a matter of individual choice, the theme of the family, the group and the community embarking on faith and commitment together is a strong one in both the Old and New Testaments. For children who live in families and within the community of the playgroup, of school, and of Sunday School, it should be a meaningful one.

Get organised

Rehearse the mime in advance if you plan to use it in *Step 2*. Think how you will organise the game in *Step 5*.

Things you may need

- [ ] the class photograph taken at last week's lesson
- [ ] brightly coloured squares of paper
- [ ] scissors
- [ ] paper plates, crayons
- [ ] date boxes, small garden sticks, papers about 8cm x 8 cm, painted or decorated
- [ ] pipe cleaners, hair nets, cardboard base, kitchen foil.

Step 1*

Talk about the pictures on page 1 of the activity paper. Some of the children will be more familiar than others with the idea of helping in a family business, especially if they have older brothers or sisters. Discuss whether they would enjoy doing this when they are older. If you discover that this is a difficult idea, talk simply about families doing things together – gardening, washing the car, and so on.

Step 2*

Tell the story of James and John on the activity paper. Again, a simple mime may be appropriate.

Explain how they worked with and for their father, as fishermen. Discuss how close their family must have been, and how important they must have been, in every way, to Zebedee. Reflect on how strongly they must have wanted to go with Jesus, and why.

Step 3*

Choose one or more of the models on page 3 of the activity paper to make with the children. If you are creating the fishing scene with nets, explain that this will be displayed on the table at worship. A piece of cardboard covered with kitchen foil could be added as a 'lake' for the boats. As you work, explain that the Lake of Galilee was huge and could be very stormy, so being a fisherman would be very hard work. Everyone would have to help.

Step 4*

If you have the photograph of your class which you took last week, show it to the children. Those who have brothers or sisters in Sunday School could identify them on the photographs of the other groups. They can tell the children what they enjoy doing with their brother or sister. You may even be fortunate enough to have twins in your class! Discuss brothers and sisters as friends, despite quarrels.

Step 5

If time and space permit, play 'Follow the Leader'.

Step 6

End by referring back to the story of James and John. Emphasise the decision they took together to follow Jesus and to have him as their leader and as their friend.

WORSHIP TIPS

Display the fishing scenes or boats.

Song

'Wherever you go I will follow', verse 2, No. 16, *Big Blue Planet*; 'I will make you fishers of men', No. 318, *Scripture Union Songs and Choruses*, 'When Jesus saw the fishermen', No. 230, *The Church Hymnary 3*.

Prayer

We thank you, Father,
for the love of friends,
for your love in Jesus
which never ends.
Amen.

Song

'He's got the whole wide world', No. 2, *Sing to God*. If you wish, use the children's names in the verses.

Bible

Last week we heard about Philip and Nathaniel and how they were friends of Jesus. Today we have heard about James and John. Philip, Nathaniel, James and John. (Children repeat the names.)

Prayer

Father God,
Thank you for the sea, the lakes and the rivers,
For fish and boats and fishermen,
Thank you for families, sisters and brothers,
For friends, for Jesus, for your love for us.
Amen.

Sickness in the family

Our goal

Our goal in this session is to portray the friendship of Jesus as whole-hearted and self-giving, and to commend his friendship as a model for living.

Bible focus

Mark 1:29–31
The generosity of Jesus' friendship is nowhere shown more strikingly than in his willingness to use his gift of healing, even on busy and stressful days. His calmness and courtesy pervade the story. In the three versions we have of it, the completeness of Peter's mother-in-law's recovery is emphasised, as is her gracious response.

Get organised

Do some research on elderly people in the congregation who are in hospital as a preparation for *Step 4*. Plan the mime in *Step 5*.

Things you may need

- ☐ crayons, card, scissors, pencils
- ☐ pipe cleaners, crêpe paper
- ☐ fresh flowers and wrapping paper
- ☐ any story appropriate to this age group about someone in hospital.

Step 1

Introduce the chosen story book, reminding the children of the story and talking about the experience of being in hospital.

Step 2*

Ask the children if they have ever been in hospital and, if so, to describe what it was like. Talk together about the good things about being in hospital: visits, gifts, and feeling very important. Also discuss the bad things: the feeling of being worried, having a pain, or missing your family.

Step 3*

Look at the pictures on page 1 of the activity paper. Encourage the children to tell the story. Discuss each picture fully, allowing them to recall experiences.

Link this to the previous discussion, reminding them of how much they looked forward to visits when they were in hospital.

Step 4*

Look at the first picture on page 3 of the activity paper. Explain that something is missing from the picture. Talk about what that might be. Encourage the children now to complete the picture, using crayons. Think together about possible gifts, and explain that when we visit people who are ill, or bring them gifts, we are showing them love and friendship.

Step 5

Make one of the gifts suggested on page 3, or have some fresh flowers and some pieces of paper to make small posies.

If possible, identify someone who might be pleased to receive the gift. If the children cannot all think of someone in their family, suggest the name of an elderly church member to print on the card and try to arrange for it to be delivered.

Step 6

Tell the story of Jesus healing Simon Peter's mother-in-law. Again, mime can be used. Emphasise that Jesus was a wonderful friend. He could also make Simon Peter's mother-in-law better. We can't do that. Doctors and nurses are in charge of making people better. But we can all show the friendship of Jesus to people who are ill or worried.

WORSHIP TIPS

Display flowers and some gifts.

Song

'Jesus' hands were kind hands', No. 228, *The Church Hymnary 3*.

Sentence

Today we have heard about an old lady who was ill. Jesus made her better. He is a wonderful friend.

Prayer

Father God
Thank you for Jesus, our wonderful friend.
We are glad to hear the story of his love.
We will try to be loving and caring like him.
Please bless our friends and anybody we love who are ill, or in bed, or in hospital.
Amen.

SESSION 4

A friend in high places

Our goal

Our goal in this session is twofold: to explain that new things happen in our lives (including new friendships) and that we should welcome these and be unafraid; and that God himself is secret and exciting.

Bible focus

John 3:1–11; 19:38–42
The quality of Jesus' life and character and the challenge and power of what he said and did attracted people of widely differing backgrounds. John gives a vivid description of Nicodemus, the man of influence and intellect, seeking out Jesus and of their conversation one evening. Jesus uses the word-picture of the wind blowing freely and without restraint to convey to Nicodemus what discipleship will mean in his life.

Get organised

Things you may need

- [ ] a seashell large enough to put to your ear
- [ ] different kinds of paper to rustle – tissue, crêpe paper, sweet wrappers, brown paper, bubble paper, newspaper
- [ ] materials for the mobile: garden cane, paper, scissors, thread, string, drawing pins
- [ ] balloons, a toy windmill, model paper or plastic planes
- [ ] materials for the kite: a piece of polythene 30 cm x 22 cm, 2 paper straws each 21 cm; scissors, sticky tape, string, thick needles, coloured tissue paper.

OFF WE GO

Step 1*

Talk about listening to the wind. Think of words like wild, strong, howling, crashing, blowing hard. Look at the picture of the trees on page 1 of the activity paper.

Listen to the sound in a shell, if you can.

Think about quieter winds blowing gently, rustling the plants and the leaves. Rustle different kinds of paper and talk about what you hear, and which kind works best.

Step 2

Make a mobile, as shown on page 1 of the activity paper. Or explain to the children that they might make one at home, as suggested on page 4 of the activity paper.

If making the mobile in class, hang it up in an outside doorway, or inside, and let the children wave their arms to make it sway. Keep this as gentle as possible!

Step 3*

Talk about how secret the wind is. You hear it but you just don't know where it is coming from, or going to. That's exciting, but sometimes quite frightening. It makes us feel that we don't know what is going to happen. It gives us a surprise, and makes us jump.

Talk about changes and new people and new things in the children's lives – a new baby, a new step-parent, a new house, a new school – and how exciting they can be.

Step 4*

Tell the story on page 2 of the activity paper, carefully making the link between Jesus' words and what the children have been learning about the wind. Explain that Jesus was telling Nicodemus that if he became his friend, new and exciting things would happen, because God – like the wind – is secret and exciting and wonderful.

Step 5*

Show the children the toys you have brought. Look together at the pictures of the wind on page 3 of the activity paper. Ask each child to pick a toy and show you the picture of it blowing in the wind.

Step 6

If time and courage permit, make the kite as shown on page 3 of the activity paper. Alternatively, show it to the children who may be able to get help at home to make the kite.

WORSHIP TIPS

Display the mobile or the toys or the kites you have made.

Song

'Wild wind blowing fresh and strong', verse 3, No. 69, *Big Blue Planet*.

Action song

(Children act the wind, blowing and swirling.)

I love the wind,
it blows round me.
God made the wind
and God made me.

Tune: 'Things I love', No. 28, *Nursery Song and Picture Book*, p. 28.

Prayer

We have been talking about the wind, Lord.
We have thought about how exciting it is.
Help us to like new and exciting things.
Teach us how exciting it is to be your friend.
Amen.

Going home

Give each child a balloon to take home.

The importance of asking questions

Our goal

Our goal in this learning session is not an easy one. It is to confront our natural wish to have answers to all of life's questions, because of the mystery and unknowability of God and of our lives.

Bible focus

John 11:6; 14:1–8; 20:24–29
Thomas can be seen either as the awkward member of the disciples or as a genuine enquirer, a seeker after truth who was not afraid to voice his doubts and his scepticism. His commitment to Jesus was deep and sincere and he has become a reassuring and encouraging figure to many people who find faith does not come easily and who have no time for blind or unthinking faith.

Get organised

Things you may need

☐ colouring pencils
☐ pictures of the natural world including a rainbow
☐ pictures of India and the people of India. (Thomas is traditionally associated with India.)

Step 1*

Talk to the children about asking questions. What do they ask questions about? Do their parents ever say: 'Stop asking questions!' Look at page 1 of the activity paper and use the ideas there to encourage discussion.

Step 2*

Tell the story of Thomas, who liked asking questions. Notice that Jesus always answered Thomas' questions: but suggest that Thomas may not have always understood the answers.

Step 3*

Link the story to page 3 of the activity paper. Talk firstly about the questions which we ask but which are not answered. Or perhaps we are told answers to our questions but we do not really understand them. Use the examples on the page but encourage the children to talk about the things which they find hard to understand.

Go on to say that the most important question of all is how we feel about Jesus. That's the wonderful thing about Thomas. Recall the story and how at the end Thomas said these words about Jesus; 'My Lord and my God'.

Step 4

Colour in the words on page 3 of the activity paper, as shown. As the children do this, say the words once or twice and try to give the children a sense of Thomas' love and friendship for Jesus.

Step 5

Learn the words of the song 'Who put the colours in the rainbow?', No. 288, *Junior Praise* or 'Who put the white in the clouds?', No. 64, *Big Blue Planet*.

Step 6*

Look at the pictures of the natural world – rainbows, animals and flowers. Ask each child to choose a favourite and to say why they have chosen it.

Step 7*

Make a rainbow. Cut strips of paper (perhaps by folding A4 paper lengthwise and cutting along the fold). Divide them into sections lengthwise and tell the children what colours to use. Then lay the papers end to end to create a long rainbow arch. Achieve a gentle curve by overlapping slightly. As you work, talk about the marvellous mystery of the rainbow.

WORSHIP TIPS

Display pictures of rainbows, animals, flowers or pictures from India. Refer to the display. If you have pictures of India, tell the children that we think that Thomas went there to tell the people about Jesus.

Song

These are songs which ask questions, questions and more questions: 'Who put the colours in the rainbow?', No 288, *Junior Praise* or 'Who put the white in the clouds?', No. 64, *Big Blue Planet*.

Prayer

Lord, you know that we are always asking questions.
Help us, like Thomas, to say to our friend Jesus
'My Lord and my God!'
Amen.
(*Children repeat the third line.*)

The man who changed his ways

Our goal

Our goal in this learning session is to show how having Jesus as a friend changes all people, and that even people we do not like or who do not treat us well can become quite different when they follow Jesus.

Bible focus

Luke 5:27–32
Both the gospels of Matthew and Mark record the story of Jesus' calling of Matthew (or Levi), the tax collector, but Luke alone tells us that Matthew 'left everything' when he followed Jesus. The change in Matthew's life was fundamental because as a tax collector his energies would have been devoted to extorting as much money as possible. When he walked out of his office, however, he started on a completely new way of life with a new direction and a new goal.

Get organised

Organise the games and the food and keep them very simple.

Things you may need

- ☐ photographs of the last Sunday School party or any party featuring children
- ☐ pencils or crayons
- ☐ music, chairs, etc., for the chosen party game
- ☐ some simple party food, for example, small cakes or biscuits, juice, plates, cups and straws
- ☐ balloons left over from Session 4.

Step 1*

Talk about people we find hard to like, and why. Use the opportunity to commend kindness and friendliness to everyone; but admit openly that some people do not treat us well, or behave badly.

The good news is that God loves everyone and that Jesus wants to be the friend of absolutely everyone, even if *we* do not think they deserve it.

Step 2*

Tell the story of Matthew on page 2 of the activity paper. Give him a big build-up as a villain; then tell very dramatically how he walked away with Jesus and was a completely different person from then on. Discuss what this tells us about Matthew and about anybody we don't like very much.

Step 3*

Recall Matthew's party. Look at the picture on page 2 again. It was a very strange party! Ask the children to recall why some people did not like having Matthew's friends there, and also to recall what Jesus said.

Step 4

If possible, look at photographs of the children at their Sunday School party. Think about parties and what happens at tea: how everyone sits round the table and enjoys cakes and ice cream, perhaps sandwiches.

Now look at page 1 of the activity paper and draw lines from the people to the places at table. The children could also draw party food on the table.

Sometimes people want to change places. Parties can cause problems! Matthew's party certainly did.

Step 5

Play a favourite party game such as 'Musical Chairs'.

Step 6*

Return to the idea of change. All about us, the world is changing all the time. Look at page 3 of the activity paper. Explain to the children how each of the living things on the left turns into something else. Take one example. Ask them to try to match the pairs. Look at the baby and then at the old man. Ask them to find out at home what *they* looked like when they were babies, and whether they have changed in that time.

Step 7*

Briefly refer to Matthew's party. Explain that Jesus was making it clear that he wanted to be the friend of every single person, good or bad. He knew that Matthew had changed and that everyone else could change too, and become better people, because Jesus had become their friend.

WORSHIP TIPS

Set out the party food and sit the children round the table. This can be done in classes, or as a whole department.

Prayer

When Jesus' friends met together, they liked having a party. We're going to have a little party today. Let's say grace first.

Father, thank you for food and for each other.
Amen.

Party Meal

Play some music and have a quick party meal.

No gift is too great

Our goal

Our goal in this session is to explore the idea of Jesus as Lord as well as friend.

Bible focus

John 12:1–8
In Matthew's gospel, as in Mark's, Jesus is anointed on the head by an unnamed woman. John's account, however, is very moving. Jesus' feet are anointed by someone who knew him well as a friend – Mary, sister of Lazarus and Martha. In this familiar setting, among well-loved friends, Mary, sensing the uniqueness of Jesus, signals her utter devotion to him as her Lord.

Get organised

Plan the mime and choose the hymns to be learned.

Things you may need

- [ ] Christmas, birthday or general gift labels, if possible with words printed on them
- [ ] materials for the banner or frieze: roll of wallpaper or frieze paper, garden canes, glue, cut-out letters or figures of children
- [ ] a story book about Paddington Bear *or* about someone having a birthday.

Step 1

Show the chosen story book to the children. If it is a Paddington Bear book, talk about the Brown family and how they welcomed Paddington into their home.

Step 2*

Ask the children whether they or anyone in their family will soon be having a birthday. Use page 1 of the activity paper to talk about gifts. Keep the discussion light-hearted and enjoy the idea of receiving and giving gifts.

Step 3

Look at some of the gift labels you have brought. Read out the captions, for example, 'With good wishes', 'With love from…', 'Merry Christmas', etc. Emphasise that gifts are a way of showing people we care for them, that they are all our friends and that we wish them well.

Step 4*

Tell the story of Mary on page 2 of the activity paper and look at the picture. If you wish, mime the story together.

Step 5*

Talk about why Mary gave this wonderful gift to Jesus and what she was trying to express to him and to her brother and sister, and to all the people who were in their home. Explain that Mary realised how special Jesus was. She knew him well. She had often spoken with him. She loved to listen to him. But still she knew he was more than just a friend. He was her Lord; when she put perfume on his feet she was praising him and telling him that she would always love and serve him.

Step 6*

As suggested on page 3 of the activity paper, make a banner or frieze to express our love and wonder that Jesus is our Lord and our friend. This will take quite some time. It should be as eye-catching and colourful as possible.
Alternatively, learn a new song about friends of God, choosing one or more of the hymns suggested below:

'Jubilate Deo', No. 2, *Big Blue Planet*
'I love you, Lord Jesus', No. 27, *Big Blue Planet*
'Praise him, praise him', No. 2, *Sing to God*
'We too would bring our treasures', verse 1, lines 5–8, No. 464,
    The Church Hymnary 3.

WORSHIP TIPS

Display the banner or frieze if one has been made.

Mary showed her love for her Lord and her friend by giving him a gift. Let us tell God how much we love him and want to be his friend.

Song

One of the hymns learned.

Prayer

Father God,
You are great and good and holy.
We worship you.
In Jesus we know your love and friendship.
Thank you for this.
Amen.

When friends let us down

Our goal

Our goal in this session is to reflect on the unhappy fact that friends can let us down, and betray our trust. We go on to commend the opposite qualities of loyalty and faithfulness in our relationships with each other and with God.

Bible focus

Matthew 26:14–16, 47–50; John 18:1–5
There is always something particularly sinister about the person who appears to be a trusted friend but who in reality is treacherous and malevolent. There have been many attempts to explain Judas' betrayal of Jesus for money but we shall never know what motivated him. The story is one of dark villainy ending in violent death. With the children, however, while confronting Judas' wrongdoing we try to take a positive line and to stress goodness and faithfulness in discipleship.

Get organised

Make a small display for the closing worship session.

Things you may need

- [ ] materials for making masks
- [ ] story book about a faithful friend, for example, about Lassie
- [ ] photographs of the children already used in Session 2
- [ ] card with caption: 'Our Friends'.

Step 1

Ask the children if they have ever had a friend who let them down or was nasty or selfish towards them. Discuss how they felt when this happened. Bring the discussion round to the idea of people being two-faced, and how we are sometimes unable to tell what people are really like, even friends.

Step 2*

Make masks together and then play the mask game.

Discuss what you have learned by playing the game. Sometimes we *think* we know what our friends are like. But sometimes they hide what they are thinking and feeling, just as they could all do when they were wearing masks. They let us down and we are hurt and angry.

Step 3*

Introduce the story of Judas by saying that Jesus had a friend like that. His name was Judas. (Children repeat the name.)

Tell the story of Judas, as shown on page 2 of the activity paper. Look at the picture. Remind the children of how dreadfully Judas let Jesus down. He did this for money. Explore the idea of using money wrongly. Link it to being greedy.

Step 4*

Look at page 3 of the activity paper. Talk about each example, selecting in particular the one which seems most appropriate to the age-group. Discuss the points suggested on the activity paper about what money can or cannot buy.

Step 5

Decorate the words of Jesus displayed in the frame. As you work, discuss what the words mean. If you like, decorate the frame with small gummed shapes.

Step 6*

Talk about friends whom we can trust and who always help us. Read the story of Lassie. Emphasise how faithful Lassie was.

WORSHIP TIPS

Display the class photographs with the caption: 'Our Friends'.

Introduction

Jesus tells us that he loves us and he wants us to be his friends.

(Refer to display.) These are pictures of lots of us here who are friends. We are also friends of Jesus.

We have been finding out from the Bible about Jesus' friends. Let's think of their names: Philip, Nathaniel, James, John, Martha, Mary, Thomas, Matthew, Nicodemus. (Allow the children, if they can, to recall the names. Prompt them by reminding them of the stories about each of the friends of Jesus. Then ask them to say their own names, adding them to the list of Jesus' friends.)

Song

'He's got the whole wide world', No. 2, *Sing to God*. Use different names in the verses. Or 'Round and round the circle', No. 22, *Big Blue Planet*. If you wish, sing this song once, then link hands and, sitting or walking, sing it again. Or 'I like to think of Jesus', No. 229, *The Church Hymnary 3*.

Prayer

Lord, we are happy to be with our friends.
We like to play and sing together.
Teach us always to be good and true.
Help us to try to be like you.
Amen.